My Big American Road Trip Coloring Book

BuzzPoP

Connect the dots to see what you'll be driving in!

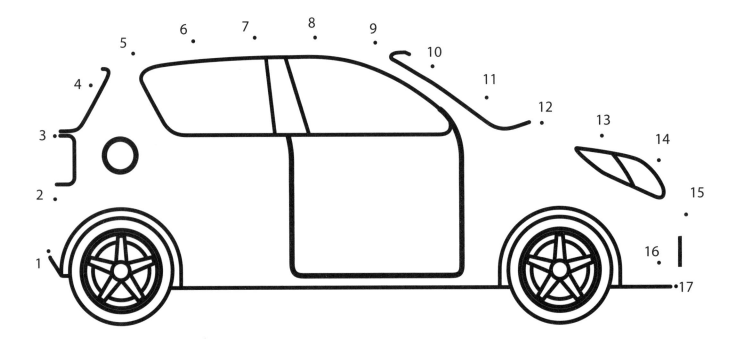

Make sure to pack plenty of snacks for the ride!

What else will you bring with you?

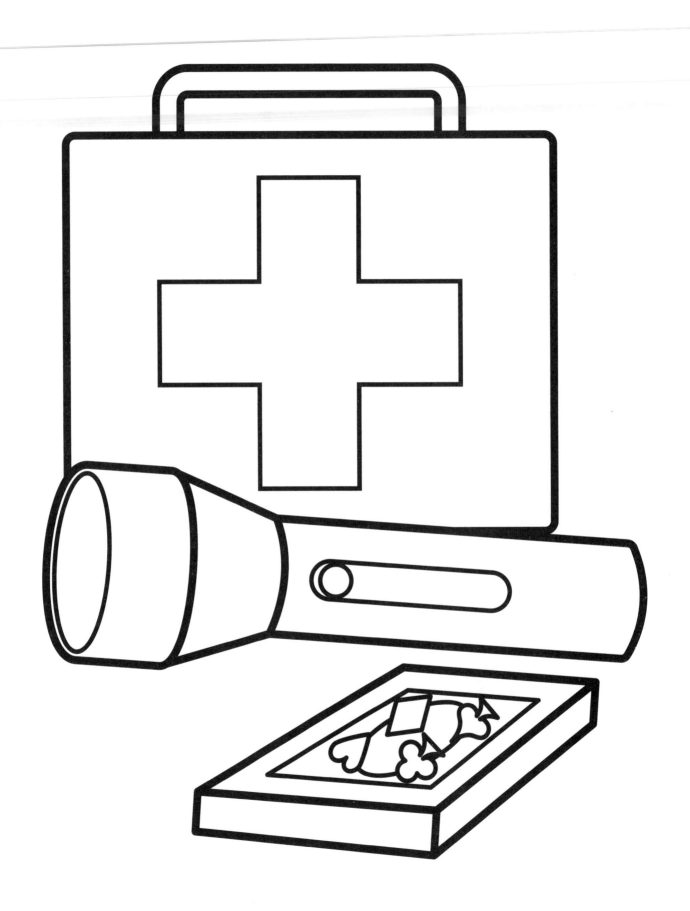

This map will help you get to your destination!

And now we're off on a big adventure!
Fill in the sign with your home state or town.

Binoculars help you spot things that are far away!

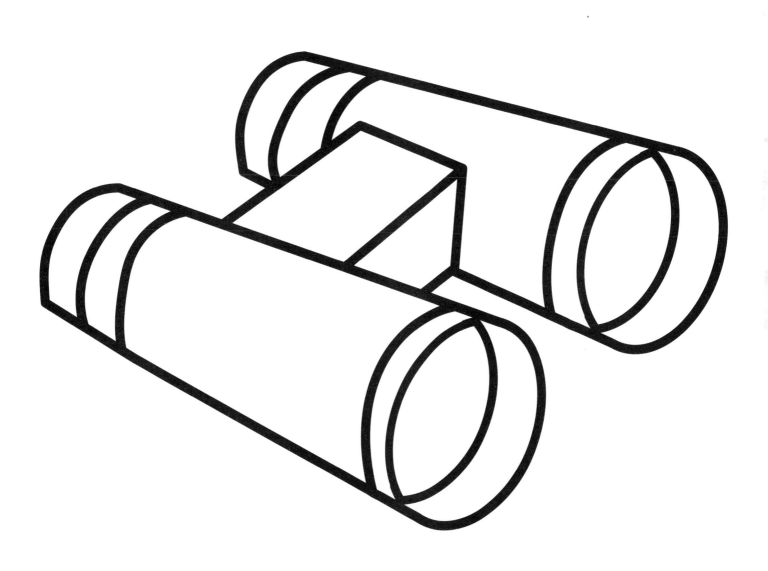

This black bear is off to find a snack!

Did you know bears eat fruit, nuts, and plants?

Wolves live in the wilderness across America!
Circle the wolf that is different from the others.

Draw what you would see out of the car window!

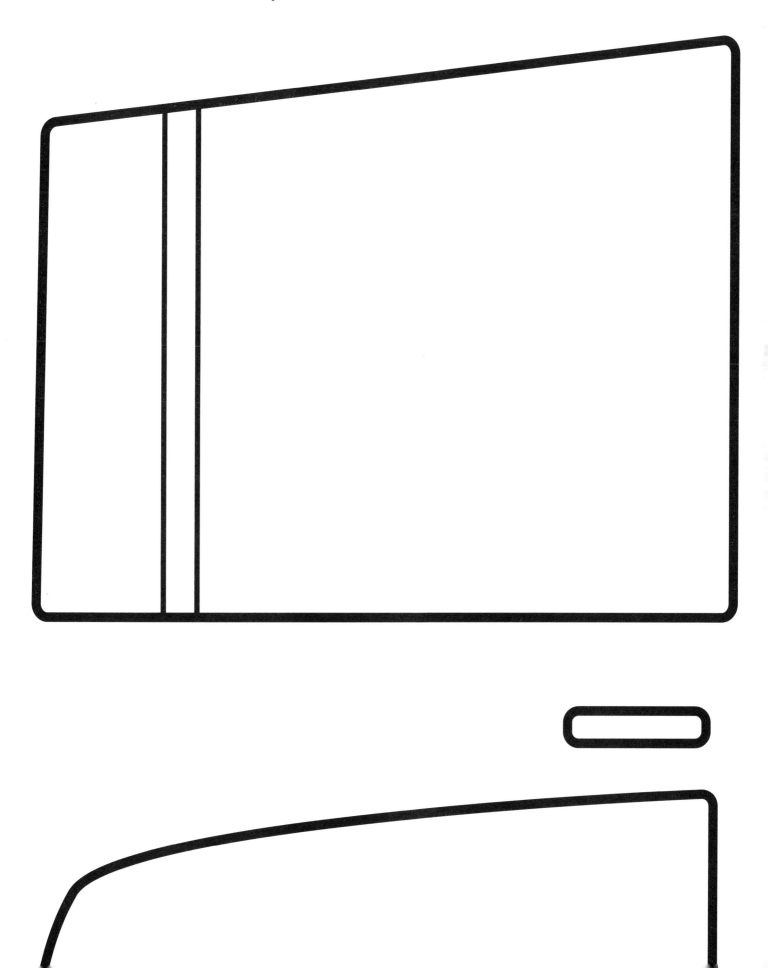

Wrigley Field is a famous baseball park!

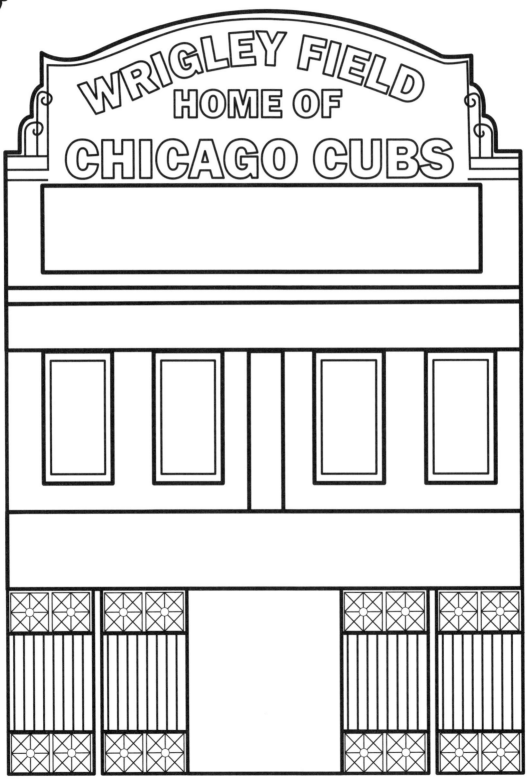

What equipment do you need to play baseball?

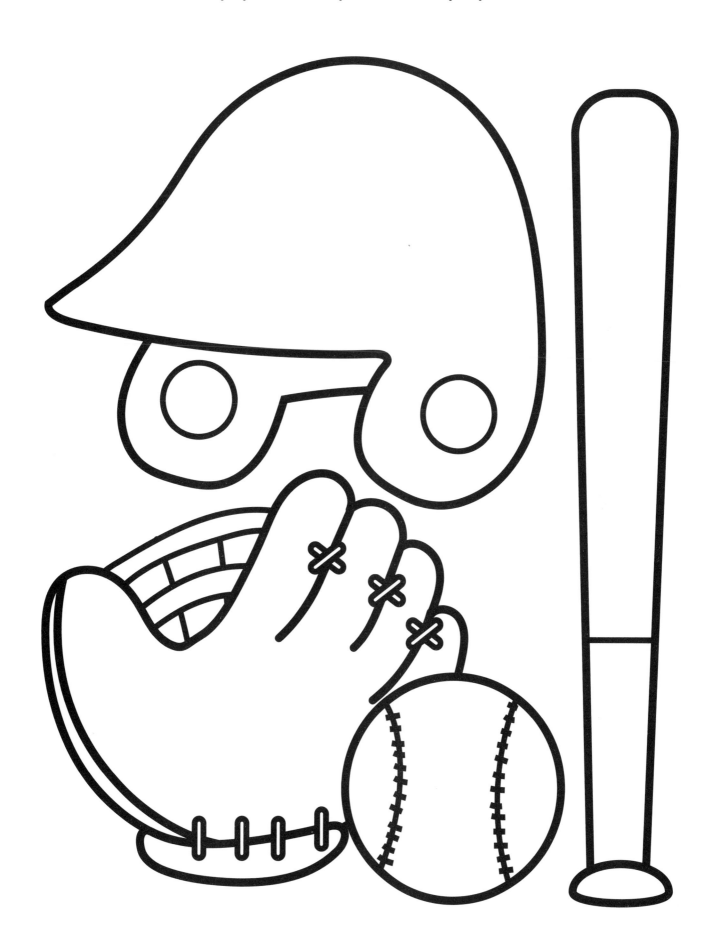

Cloud Gate is known to many as "the bean" and is located in Millennium Park in Chicago!

IL

Did you know that the cardinal is
the state bird of Illinois?

IL

We are now passing through a town called Santa Claus! It's in Indiana.

Peony plants can live to be 100 years old!

Did you know that horses can sleep lying down or standing up?

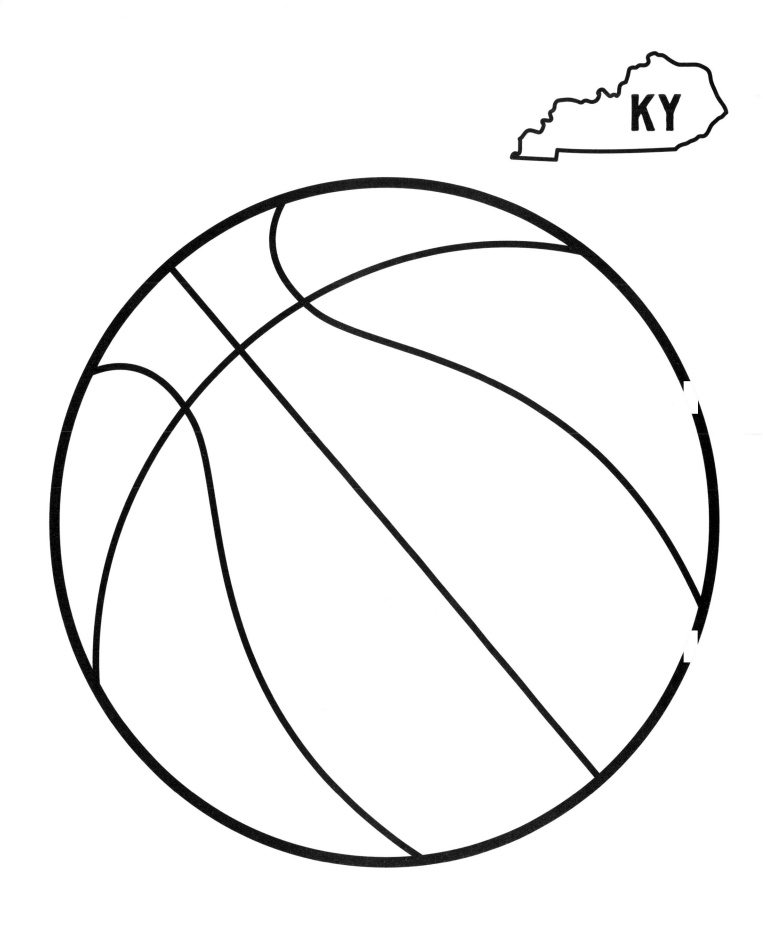

Kentucky is famous for college basketball!

Connect the dots to reveal a tasty snack!

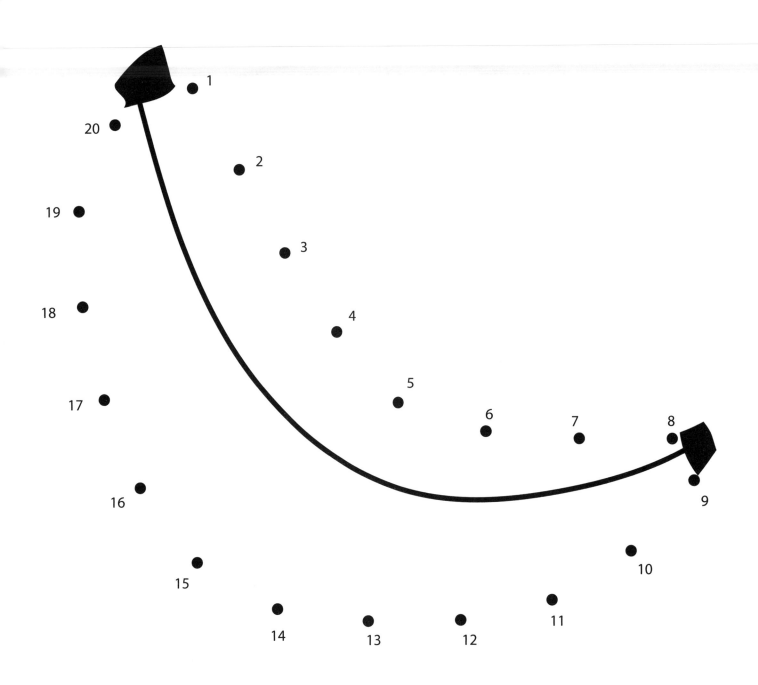

Carnations are Ohio's official state flower!

Let's rock!
Ohio has the Rock & Roll Hall of Fame.

Hop! Hop! Hop! Did you know baby rabbits are called "kittens"?

Botanical gardens are a great place to view and learn about plants!

Does this remind you of a vegetable? It's an island off the shore of Michigan in Lake Huron. It's called Turnip Rock!

Robins are Michigan's state bird!

Lake Champlain sits among Vermont, New York, and Canada!

There may be a monster lurking in Lake Champlain. Locals call him Champ!

How many fish do you spot in this river?
Your answer:____

Vermont is famous for its ice cream!
What's your favorite flavor?

VT

Can you match each animal to its name?

Wolf

Moose

Bear

Farmers' markets are a great way to support local farms!

Moose antlers can reach up to six feet end to end!

How about taking the Cog way to
the summit of Mount Washington?
It's one of New Hampshire's greatest attractions!

Bobcats can run up to 30 miles per hour,
but they prefer walking!

The purple lilac is the official state flower of New Hampshire!

NH

Help the beaver get back to its dam!

It's a great day for a ferry ride!

Welcome to Acadia National Park!

ME

**Did you know that Maine's
state flower is a white pine cone,
even though it isn't actually a flower?**

Maine is known for lobsters!

Maine is home to the world's largest rotating globe!
It's called Eartha.

Mount Katahdin is the highest mountain in Maine and at the end of the Appalachian Trail!

Racoons are nocturnal, meaning they're only active at night!

Can you match each snack to its name?

Chips

Popcorn

Apple

Boston is home to America's first lighthouse!

Hope you had a wheel-y nice time!

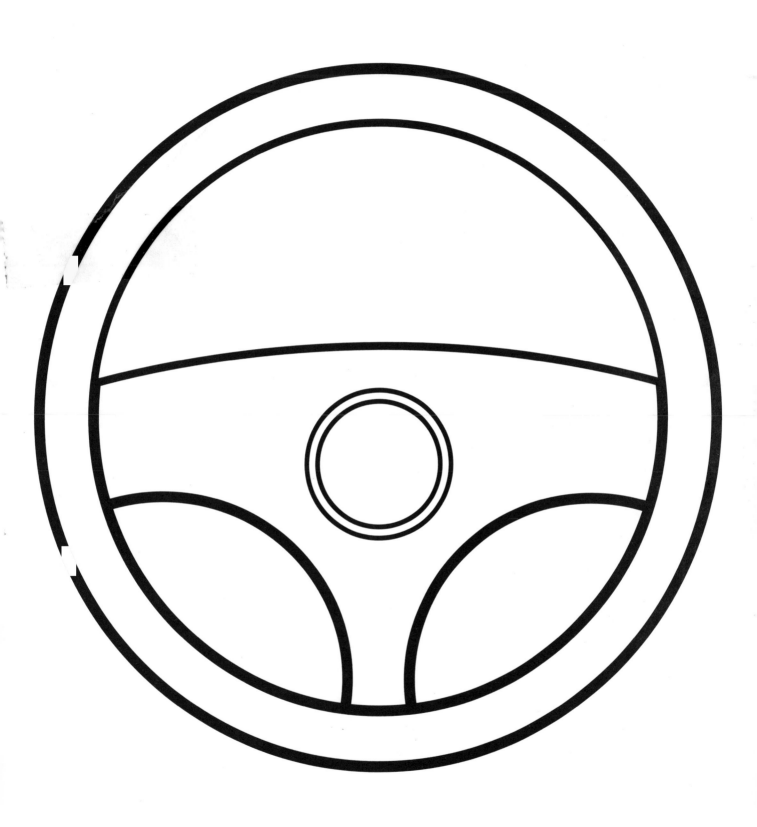

Here's a look at where we've been.

You've made it back home! Fill in the sign with your home state or town.

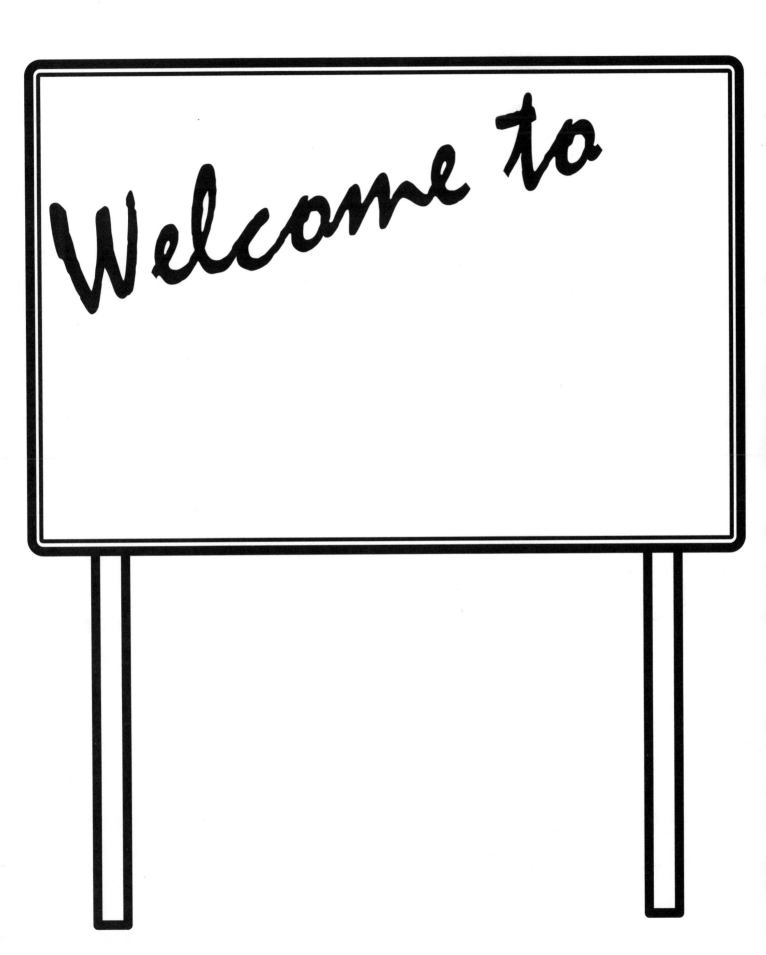

The highway sure looks busy!

Circle the truck that has the most wheels!

Fill in this photo of your favorite part of the trip!

It seems there's some roadwork up ahead, so let's take a detour!

Whew, that was close! Let's get back on the road.

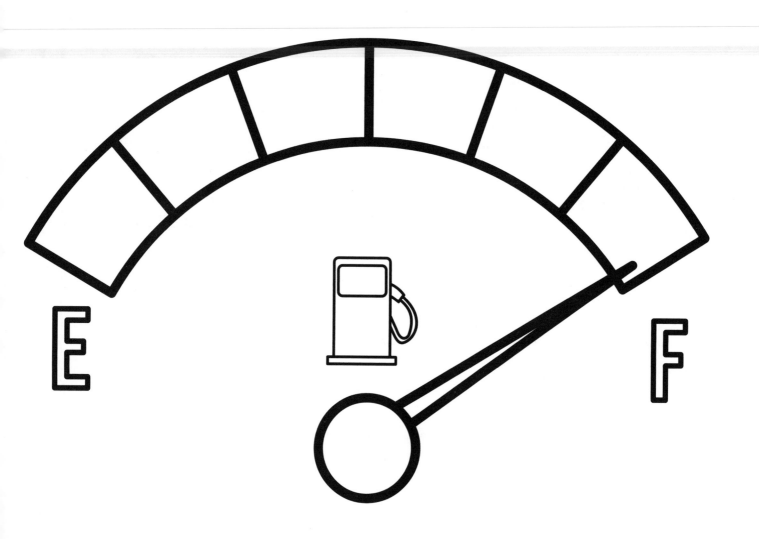

Help the car get to the gas station!

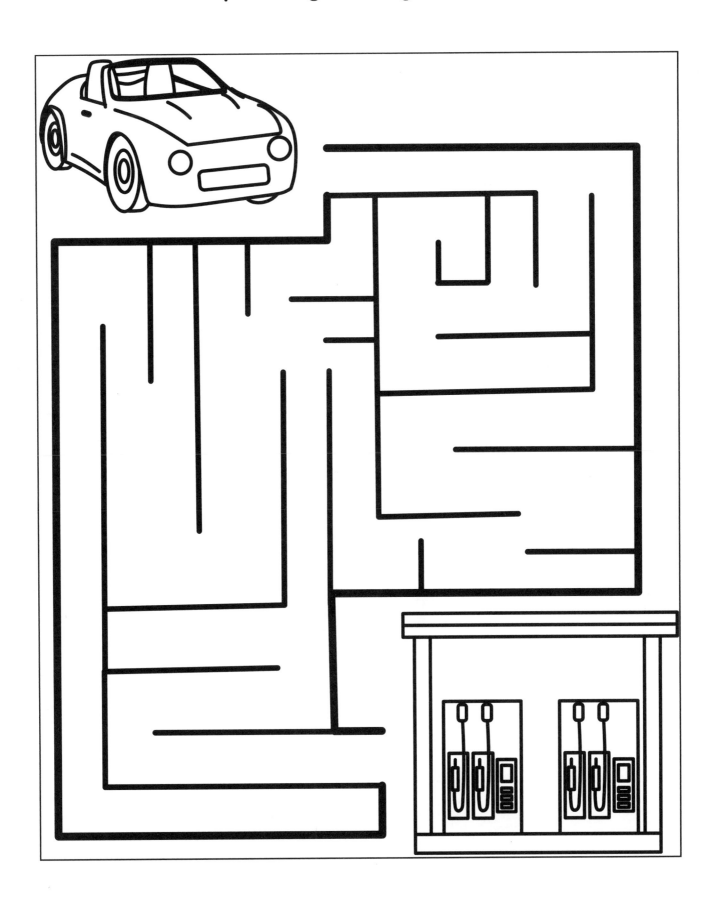

Check the car's gas gauge. Uh, oh. It's on E!

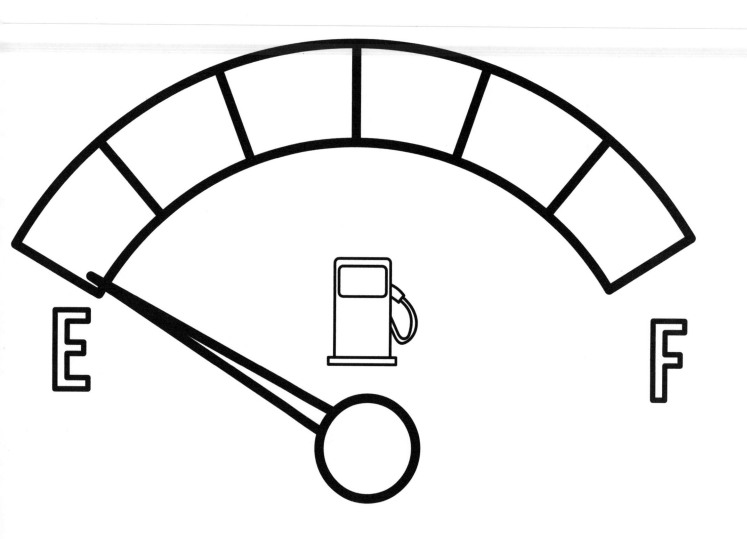

Pee-yew! That skunk is cute, but smelly!

Can you match each animal to its name?

Fox

Snake

Owl

Do you like to go camping? Color the picture in to make your perfect tent!

Wisconsin has a lot of dairy farming!

Minnesota is home to Superior National Forest and the International Wolf Center.

Iowa has nine types of bats!
This one is a little brown bat.

IA

Have you heard of Elwood?
He's the world's tallest concrete gnome!
He can be found in Iowa.

Chirp! Chirp!
**Did you know crickets listen with tiny
ears they have on their legs ?**

There's plenty of wildlife to
see in Lone Elk Park!

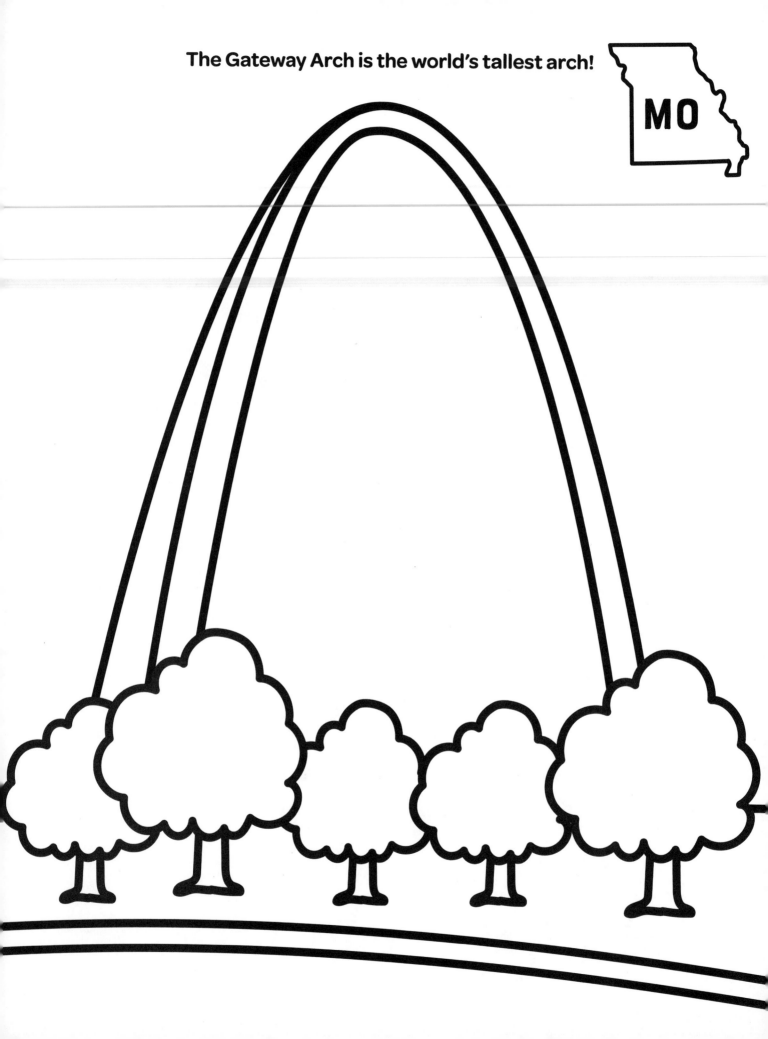

MO

Did you know Missouri is home to the
world's second-largest rocking chair?

How about stopping to see Missouri's fantastic caverns?

KS

Armadillos can be found in Kansas!
Their name comes from the Spanish work *armado*, which means *"armed."*

Did you know that Kansas has eight wonders?
One of these is the Monument Rocks.

KS

NE

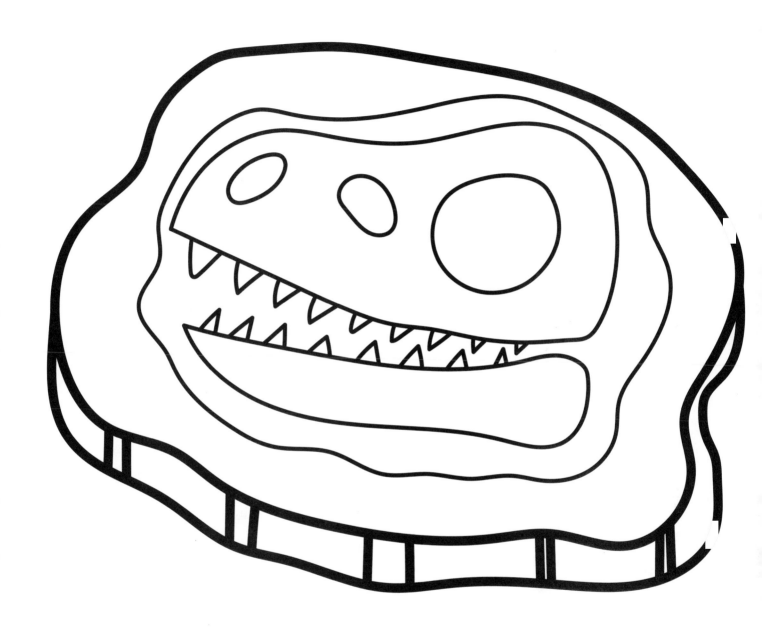

Fossils are awesome! The Ashfall Fossil Beds in Nebraska have fossils of animals who lived over 12 million years ago.

Nebraska's state insect is the honeybee!

SD

South Dakota is home to nine tribes of Indigenous peoples.

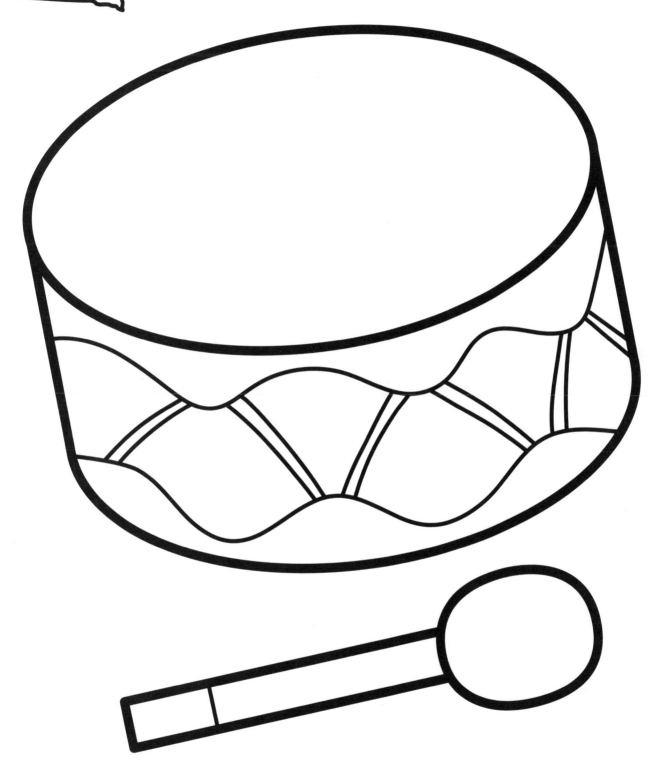

The Mount Rushmore National Memorial carved into the mountains in the Black Hills region of South Dakota depicts U.S. presidents George Washington, Thomas Jefferson, Theodore Roosevelt, and Abraham Lincoln.

Help the prairie dog get to the grass!

You can find prairie dogs in the
Badlands National Park in South Dakota.

ND

The overlook at the Painted Canyon Visitor Center gives you a great sight of the Badlands!

North Dakota is the number-one producer of honey in America!

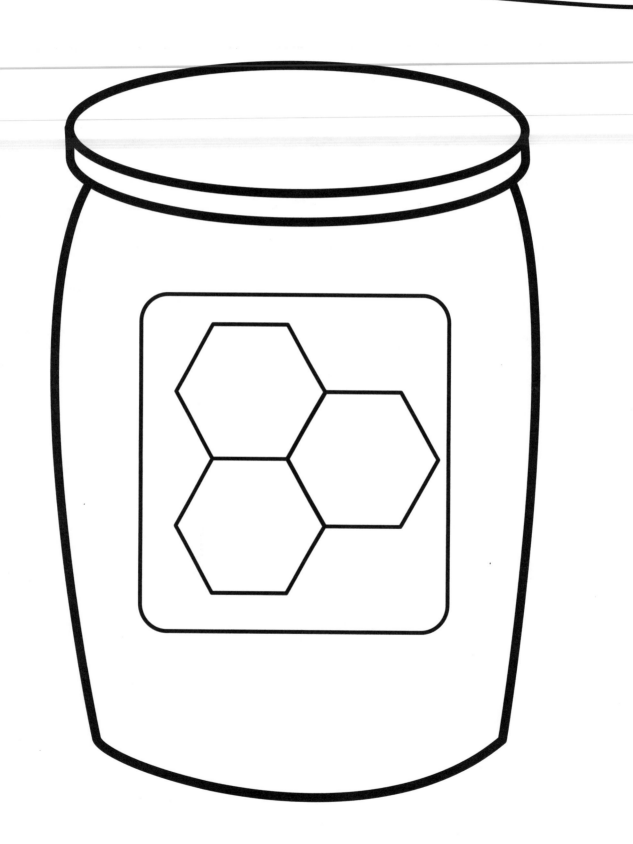

ID

A college football game between the
University of North Dakota and Idaho State
is called the Potato Bowl USA!

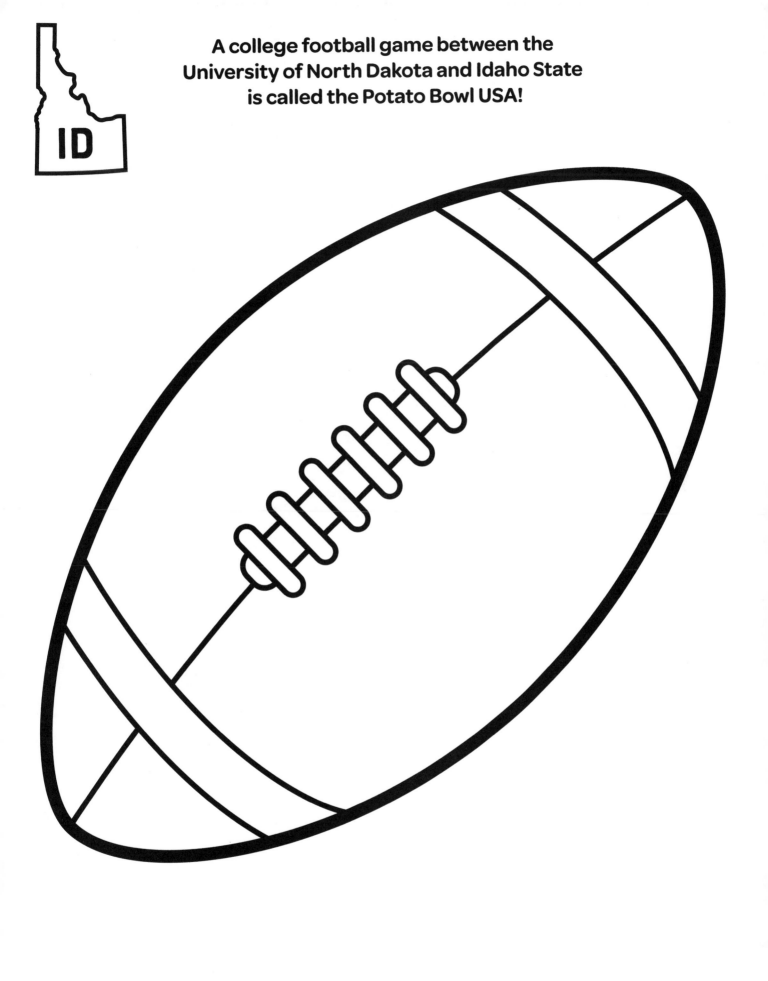

Bald eagles have an average wingspan of 7 feet!

It's a field of wildflowers! Color each flower a different color.

Circle the tree that is different from the others!

MT

Yip! Yip! Did you know coyotes are good swimmers?

This grizzly bear is fast!
Did you know they can run up to 30 miles per hour?

Glacier National Park

MT

Circle the animal that doesn't live in Yellowstone!

How many bison do you see in the field?
Your answer:____

The bison is America's national animal and largest land mammal!

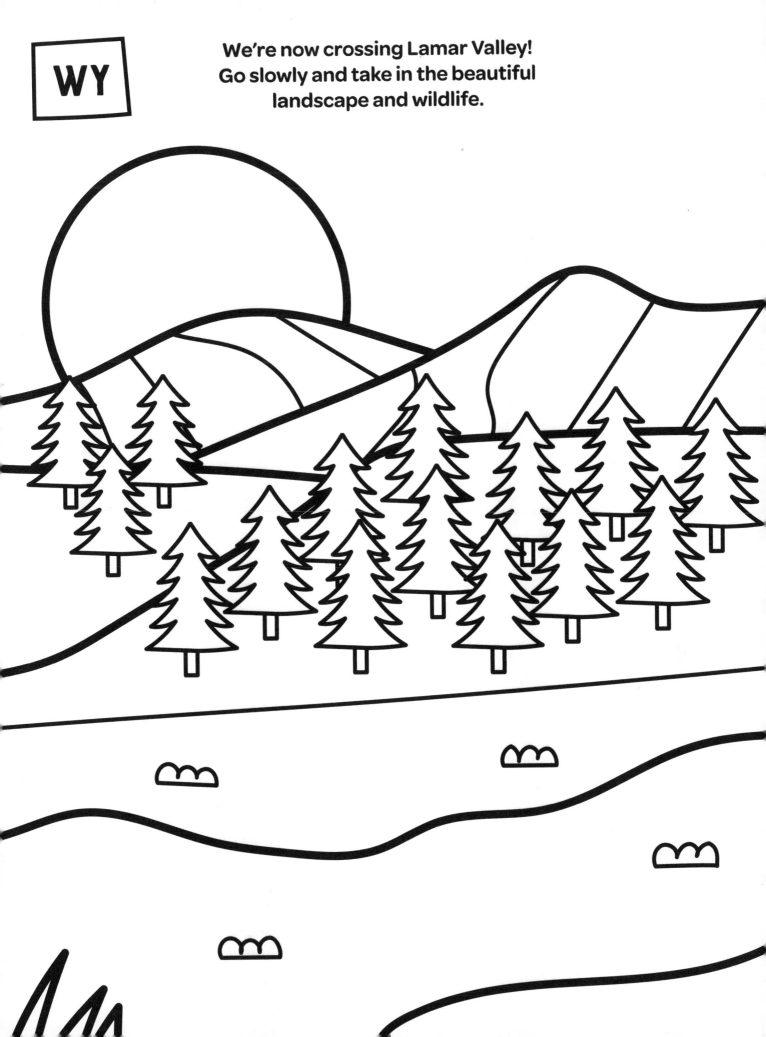

We're now crossing Lamar Valley!
Go slowly and take in the beautiful
landscape and wildlife.

It's the Old Faithful Geyser, one of Yellowstone's most iconic landmarks!
A geyser is a vent in earth's surface! It blasts water 130 feet in the air!

Don't forget to fill your backpack with what you need!

What would you want your hiking boots to look like? Color them in!

It's time to stretch your legs! Let's go on a hike.

See that mountain? It's the iconic Washington landmark Mount Rainier. It's a stratovolcano!

Washington's State bird is the American goldfinch!

Help the bald eagle get to her nest! Bald eagles are the United States of America's national bird.

WA

The Space Needle is a 605-foot-tall spire located in Seattle, Washington!

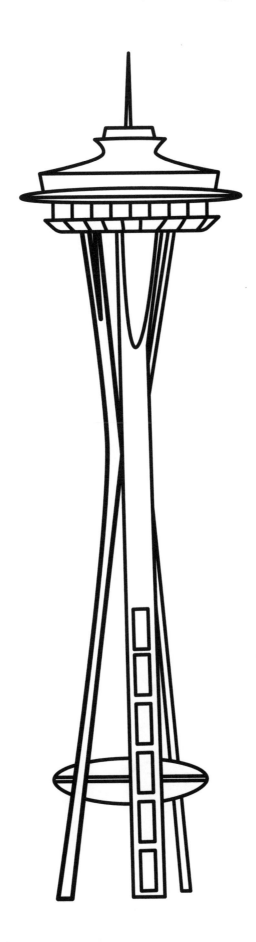

OR

Crater Lake was formed due to
the collapse of volcano Mount Mazama!

Do you recognize this rock?
This landmark, Haystack Rock, is one of the
most popular attractions in Oregon!

OR

WA

**Keep your eyes peeled
for the elusive Northern Pygmy-Owl!**

There are 14 different kinds of snakes that can be located in Sequoia National Park!

CA

The California poppy is a beautiful flower!

CA

How many monarch butterflies can you find?
Your answer:____

General Sherman Tree is the largest tree in the world. It's a giant sequoia!

Ding! Ding!
Did you know that San Francisco's cable car system is the world's last manually operated cable car system?

CA

Let's travel north to see
the Golden Gate Bridge.
It's over a mile and a half long!

CA

**Look—it's the Half Dome!
It's known for its distinct shape.**

CA

That large rock formation is called El Capitan.
It's popular amongst rock climbers!

CA

Let's go for a bike ride. Don't forget your helmet!

Yosemite Falls is the highest waterfall in Yosemite!

CA

Of all the palm trees in Los Angeles, only one species is native to California!

CA

How about a spin on the Merry-Go-Round?

Write your name in this star for the Hollywood Walk of Fame!

Can you see the Hollywood sign on the hill?

Surf's up! Decorate the surfboard using different colors.

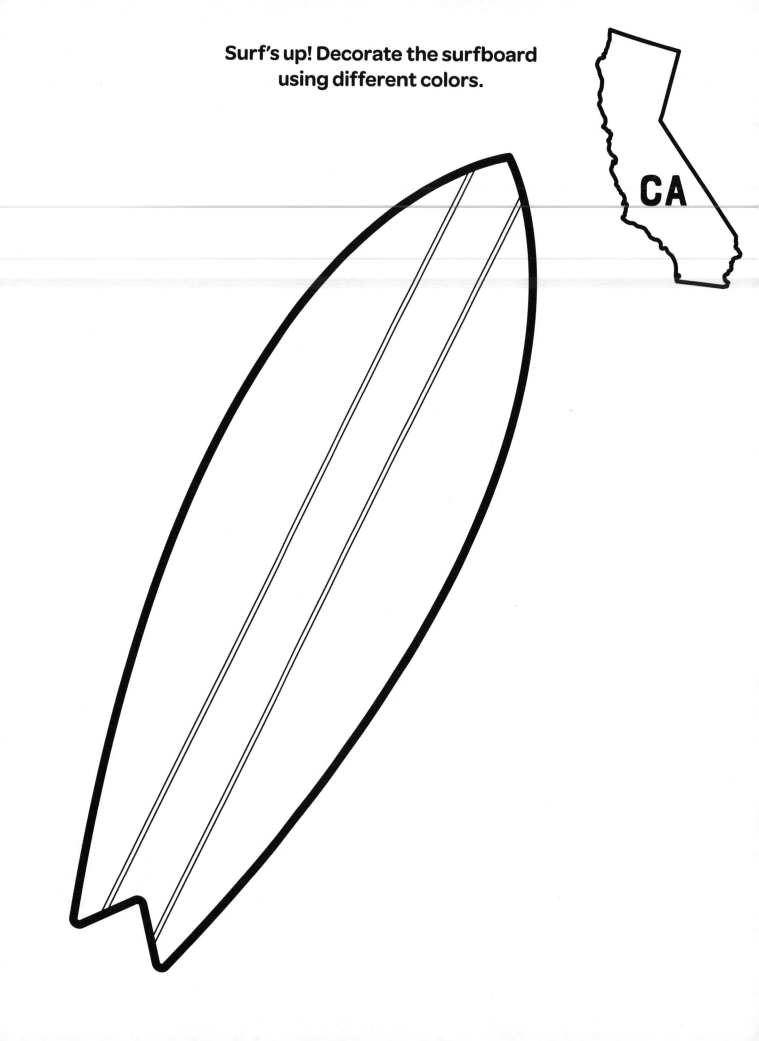

Look! There's a dolphin!

The Santa Monica Pier looks out to the Pacific Ocean on the West Coast!

It's relaxing at the beach!

The Hoover Dam is used to generate electricity for people in Arizona, Nevada, and California!

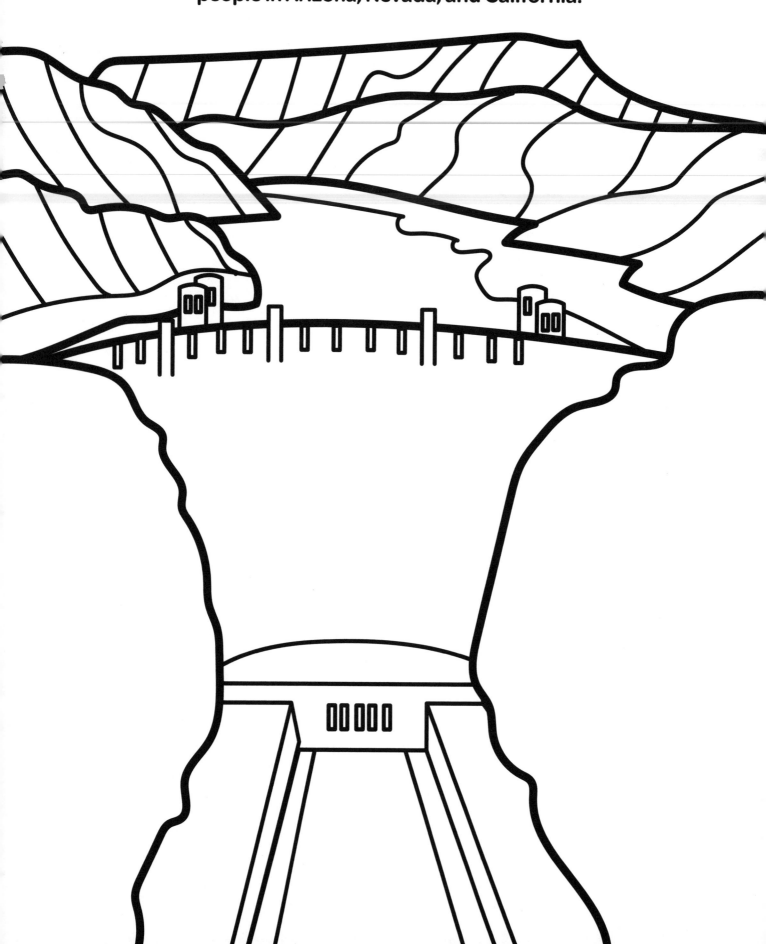

The Grand Canyon is 277 miles long
and 18 miles wide!

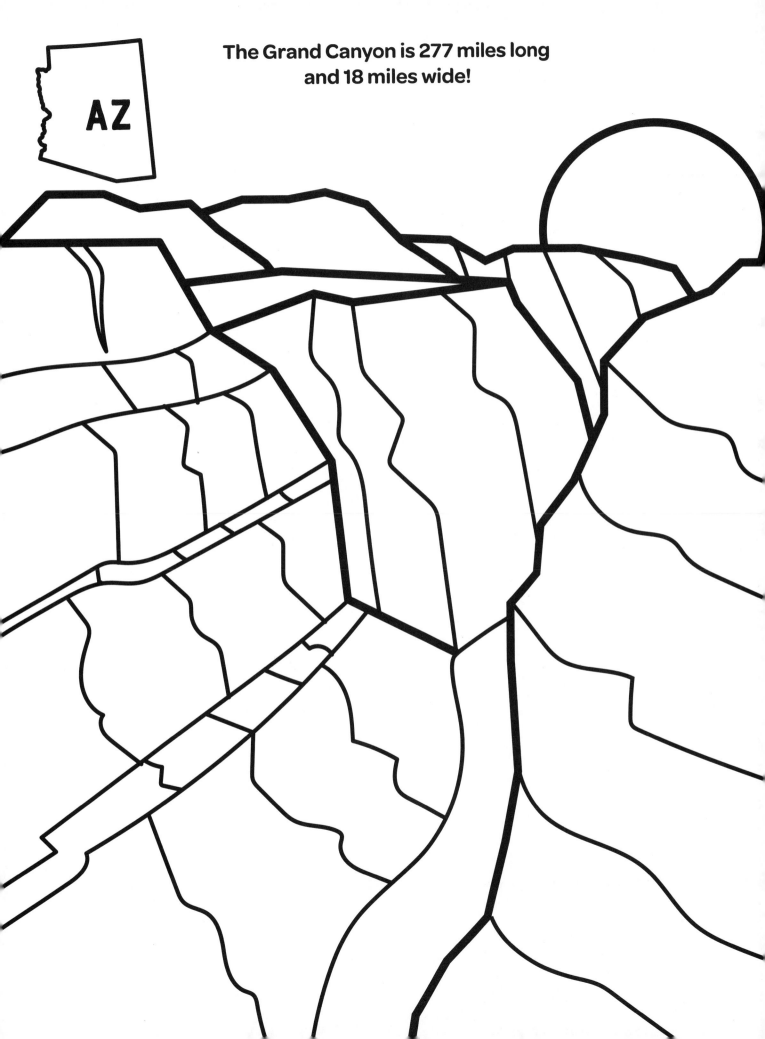

Welcome to the Navajo Nation's
Monument Valley Park!
Its Navajo name is Tsé Bii' Ndzisgaii.

AZ

**Chuckwallas are members of the iguana family.
They can be found in the Arizona desert!**

AZ

The state flower of Arizona
is the white blossom of the saguaro—
the largest cactus in the United States!

AZ

How about going on a UFO tour?
Alien sightings have been reported in New Mexico!

Take in the Rocky Mountain scenery at Maroon Bells-Snowmass Wilderness!

CO

Cowabunga!
Go sand sledding at the
Great Sand Dunes National Park and Preserve!

Let's go white water rafting in the Colorado River!

CO

CO

In Colorado, you can take a tour led by a park ranger in Mesa Verde National Park to see Cliff Palace!

Take in the sights of the Taos Pueblo!
It's one of the oldest inhabited
communities in the U.S.

NM

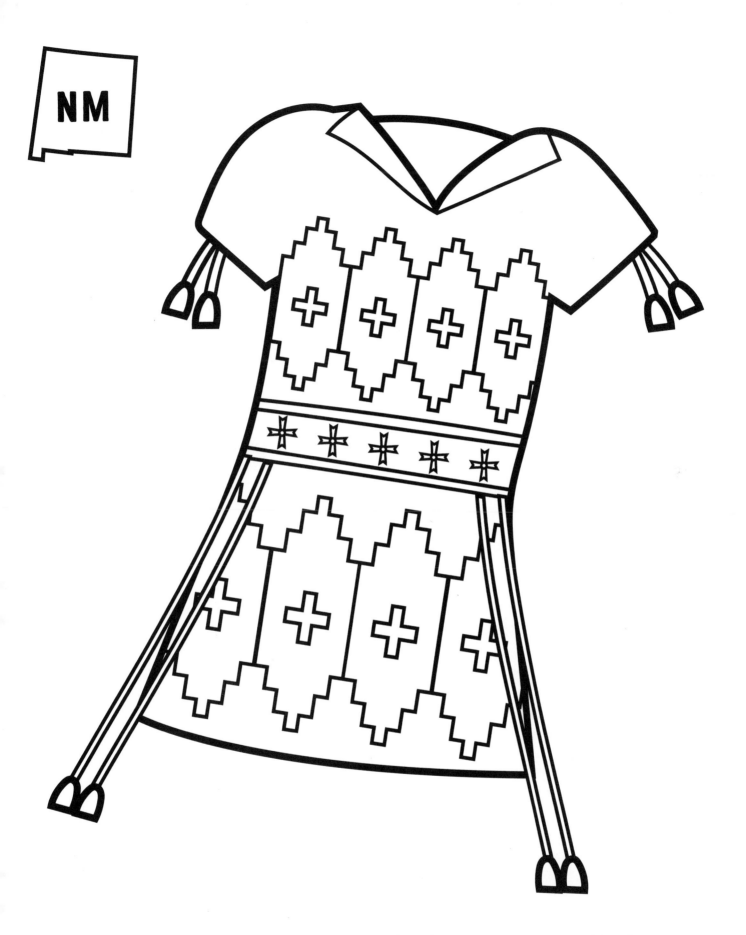

**The Gathering of Nations is held in Albuquerque, New Mexico.
It is the largest powwow in the United States!**

Texas is famous for its barbecue!

The Alamo is a historic Spanish mission and the site of the Battle of the Alamo.

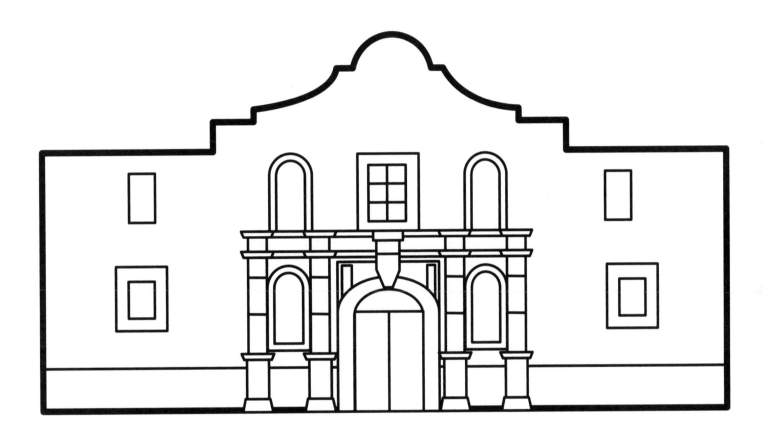

Oklahoma's state tree is the redbud!

The Blue Whale of Catoosa was built in 1972.

The white-tailed deer is the state mammal of Arkansas!

Welcome to the Arkansas River Valley!
Let's go fishing.

AR

MI

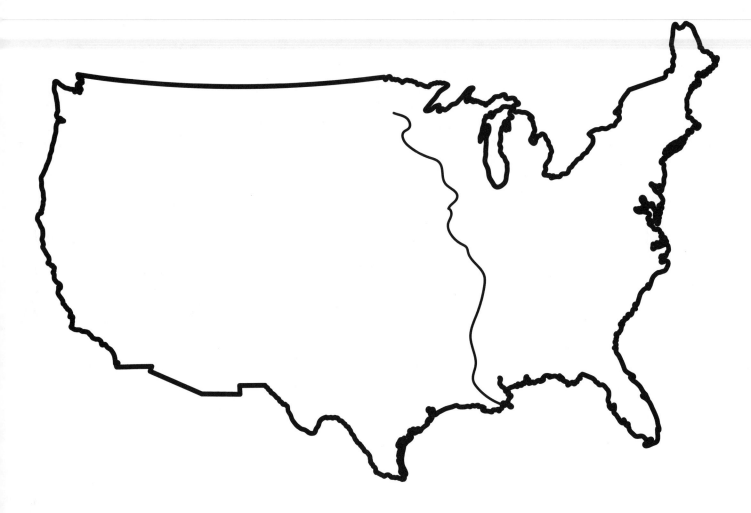

**The Mississippi River is the second-longest river in America.
It runs through ten states!**

Do you like ducks?
One of Mississippi's state birds is the wood duck!

Connect the dots to see a prickly plant that can be found in hot, dry climates!

**Louisiana is a beautiful state.
Let's go on a shrimp boat tour out of New Orleans!**

**Stop and smell the flowers.
Alabama's state flower is the camellia!**

Flamingos are social birds and live in colonies!

Ribbit! Ribbit! Frogs love hopping!

FL

Snorkeling is a fun way to view sea life
in its natural habitat.

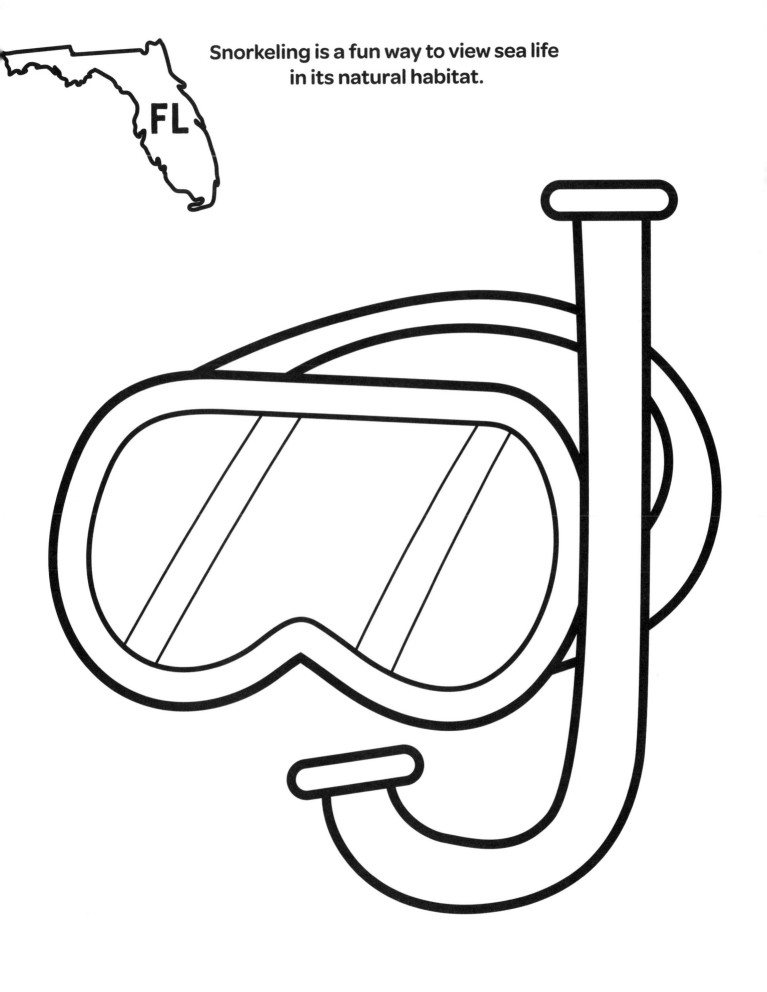

Look!
Someone is paddleboarding.

Can you spot the alligator?

Welcome to the Everglades! Here, you can find the endangered leatherback turtle.

How many alligators can you see in this swamp? Your answer: ____

Look at the beautiful magnolia tree! Magnolias represent endurance and long life.

GA

Did you know Florida is also called the Sunshine State?

Let's visit the birthplace of Martin Luther King, Jr. in Atlanta!

MARTIN LUTHER KING, JR. WAS BORN IN THIS HOUSE JANUARY 15, 1929

Georgia is famous for its peaches!

GA

Draw your favorite sea animal above!

GA

The trees on Driftwood Beach are beautiful.

The Georgia Aquarium is the largest in the world!
What's your favorite sea creature?

SC

River otters live in rivers, marshes, and ponds, making South Carolina's coast a great home!

Did you know there are eleven types of herons that can be found in both North and South Carolina?

SC

Horses are roaming the fields in the Great Smoky Mountains!
This forest is on the border of Tennessee and North Carolina.

The Shenandoah Valley in Virginia is nicknamed "The Big Valley."

Let's float down the river in an inner tube. Don't forget your life vest!

The New River Gorge Bridge is the third-longest single arch bridge in the world!

Oak trees are one of the oldest trees on the planet.
They can live up to 1,000 years!

About six million people visit the
Lincoln Memorial every year!

DC

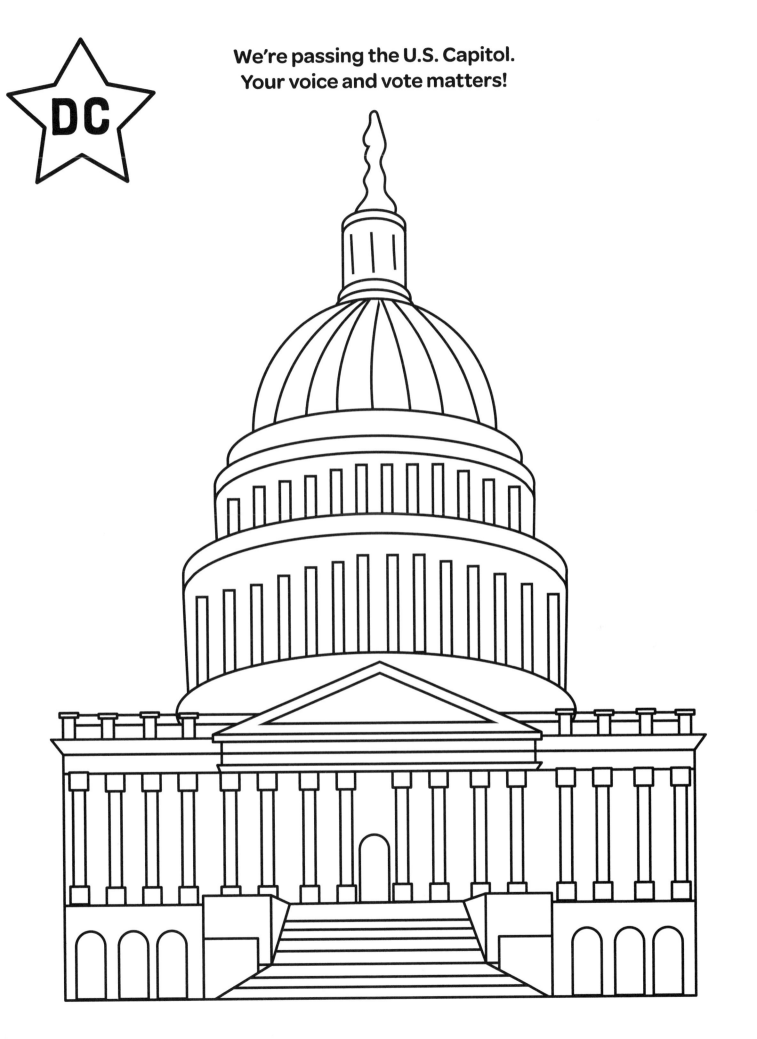

We're passing the U.S. Capitol.
Your voice and vote matters!

DC

Maryland is known for its blue crabs found in Chesapeake Bay.

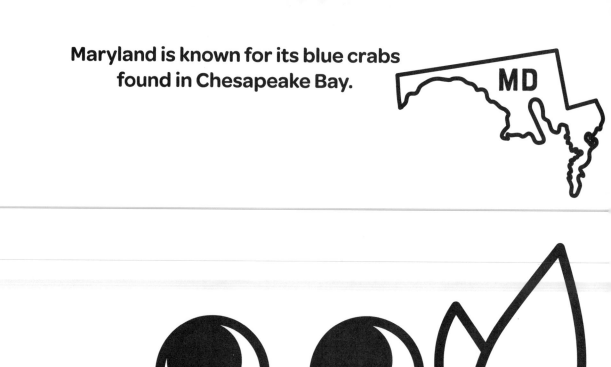

The Baltimore oriole is Maryland's state bird!

We're back on the road! What's your favorite music to listen to?

Choo! Choo! Go for a ride on the Wilmington and Western Railroad! It's a historic place in Delaware.

DE

70

Atlantic City has a popular boardwalk.

NJ

Let's check out some arcade games!

Decorate this sandcastle!

Let's go down the shore!

New Jersey is also known as the Garden State thanks to its farmers!

NJ

New York City's pizza is delicious!

Did you know New York's state flower is the rose?

NY

Oh, look. There's the Statue of Liberty!

New York is a great place to see a play or a show!

There are a lot of pigeons in New York City!

NY

The Empire State Building has 102 floors!

New York's nicknamed the Big Apple!
What's your nickname?

Wow! Niagara Falls sure is beautiful!

NY

The Liberty Bell is a symbol of freedom. It's one of America's biggest attractions!

Roar!
The Philadelphia Zoo is the oldest zoo in the U.S.

Did you know that lobsters shed their shells each year and grow a new one?

A traditional clambake includes corn on the cob, potatoes, clams, and lobster.

PA

Sample some chowder recipes and help determine who has the best chowder in New England!

Did you know that opossums have great memory?

We're now passing through Cape Cod.
Keep your eye out for Salty the Seahorse.
He's 38 feet tall!

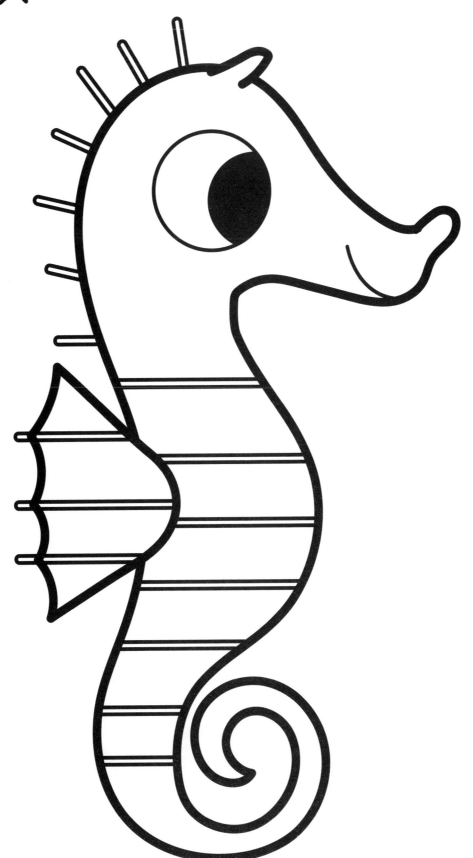

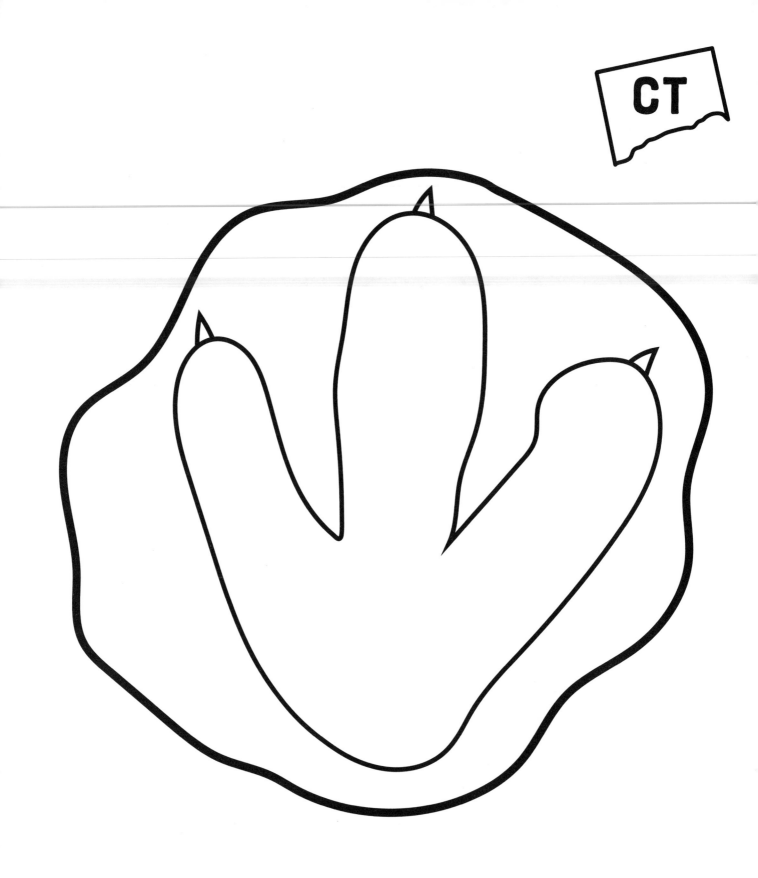

That's a dinosaur footprint! Did you know that there are hundreds of dinosaur tracks along the Connecticut River?

Draw your own dinosaur!

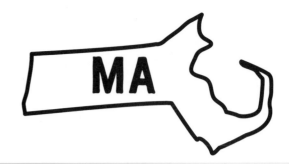

Whale watching is fun!
This is a humpback whale.